APPLIQUÉ
Inside the Lines

Carol Armstrong

12 QUILT PROJECTS TO EMBROIDER & APPLIQUÉ

C&T PUBLISHING

© 2003, Carol Armstrong

Editor-in-Chief: Darra Williamson

Editor: Pamela Mostek

Technical Editor: Pamela Mostek

Copy Editor: Lynn Koolish

Proofreader: Susan Nelsen

Cover Designer: Christina Jarumay

Book Designer: Rose Sheifer

Design Director: Rose Sheifer

Illustrator: Kate Reed

Production Assistant: Jeff Carillo

Photography: Sharon Risendorph

Digital Photography: Diane Pedersen

Published by C&T Publishing, Inc., P.O. Box 1456,
Lafayette, California 94549

Front cover: Fresh Fruit
Back cover: Blue Ribbon Bouquet, Gold Pepper Berries, Floral Butterflies

Attention Teachers: C&T Publishing, Inc. encourages you to use this book as a text for teaching. Contact us at 800-284-1114 or www.ctpub.com for more information about the C&T Teachers' Program.

We take great care to ensure that the information included in this book is accurate and presented in good faith, but no warranty is provided nor results guaranteed. Since we have no control over the choices of materials or procedures used, neither the author nor C&T Publishing, Inc. shall have any liability to any person or entity with respect to any loss or damage caused directly or indirectly by the information contained in this book. For your convenience, we post an up-to-date listing of corrections on our web page (www.ctpub.com). If a correction is not already noted, please contact our customer service department at ctinfo@ctpub.com or at P.O. Box 1456, Lafayette, CA 94549.

Trademarked (™) and Registered Trademark (®) names are used throughout this book. Rather than use the symbols with every occurrence of a trademark and registered trademark name, we are using the names only in the editorial fashion and to the benefit of the owner, with no intention of infringement.

Library of Congress Cataloging-in-Publication Data

Armstrong, Carol
  Appliqué inside the lines : 12 quilt projects to embroider & appliqué / Carol Armstrong.
     p. cm.
Includes index.
  ISBN 1-57120-189-0 (paper trade)
  1. Appliqué--Patterns. 2. Embroidery--Patterns. 3. Quilts.
I. Title.
  TT779 .A75797 2003
  746.44'5041--dc21
                               2002013371

Printed in China
10 9 8 7 6 5 4 3 2 1

Table

Introduction 5

Getting Started 6

Supplies 6

Techniques 9

Finishing 14

# of Contents

Blue Ribbon Bouquet 18   Fish Are A-Swimmin' . . .38   Vanilla Leaves 58

Gold Pepper Berries 22   Roses Are Red 44   Dresden Plate 62

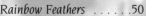

Golden Stars 26   Rainbow Feathers 50   Floral Butterflies 66

Six in Bloom 30   Basic Black and White . . .54   Fresh Fruit 70

Quilting Designs 76
About the Author 78
Index 79

This book is dedicated to
other needlework lovers who
share my enjoyment of
stitching something beautiful.

INTRODUCTION

Remember back to the joys of a coloring book and a box of colored crayons? Now you can have that same fun by drawing pictures with embroidered lines and coloring inside the lines with fabrics, from rainbow brights to dramatic black and whites. With this exciting combination of simple embroidery and basic appliqué, it couldn't be easier or more fun to recreate that look.

This technique is excellent for beginners and offers new direction and inspiration for experienced stitchers. It's also a great chance for those of you who are appliqué fans to add another technique to your bag of tricks! And the same is true for embroidery lovers. Have you thought of adding appliqué to your embroidery projects? I think you'll be very pleased with the results.

Any favorite design or theme can be adapted for this combined technique of embroidery and appliqué. For inspiration, go back to those children's coloring books. They're a great place for fun ideas. Or take a look at stained glass designs. Traditional quilting block designs, such as *Dresden Plate*, page 62, or quilting designs such as *Rainbow Feathers*, page 53, also lend themselves to outlines filled with color.

And color itself can change any design. Play with different background colors and experiment with different shades of embroidery floss. Try different fabrics for your appliqué designs. Prints and solids, darks and lights can all combine for stunning effects.

Go ahead and give it a try. You'll feel like a kid again!

Happy Stitching,

Carol Armstrong

Carol Armstrong

Getting Started

*H*ere you'll find everything you'll need to know to make the fourteen delightful quilts in this book. From needles to fabric, I've included helpful information on choosing and gathering your supplies. Next, you'll find tips and instructions on the techniques you will use in this exciting new process of combining embroidery and appliqué. Finally, I've shared my favorite methods for finishing your quilt. Before you get started on your favorite *Appliqué Inside the Lines* project, read through the tips and suggestions in this section, and you'll be ready to start creating!

SUPPLIES...what you'll need

NEEDLES

A large-eyed embroidery needle is best for embroidery. I use size 8. The larger eye will make threading several strands of floss onto the needle easier. Appliqué stitching is best done with a longer milliners' needle (size 10). The added length helps in turning under the allowance as you stitch. A sharps size 10 is my favorite for quilting and piecing, or you may prefer the shorter "between" needle for quilting. Give them both a try.

PINS

Short glass-headed pins work well for holding appliqué pieces in place as you sew. These pins that are only ¾" long are less likely to get in the way as you stitch. Standard silk pins are handy when piecing, adding borders, and binding. Discard any bent or burred pins to avoid pulling threads.

MARKING TOOLS

Be sure to select markers that are easily removed from fabrics. The readily available blue water-removable markers work well for both marking embroidery designs and quilting designs on most fabrics. For marking dark fabrics try white fabric pencils. Test your chosen marker on fabric to ensure it will go away when you're ready. Be sure to avoid ironing marker lines by removing them before you press.

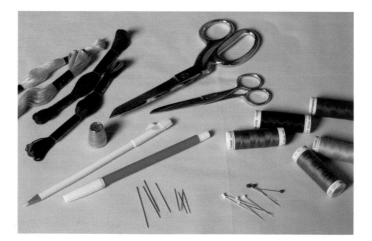

LIGHTBOX

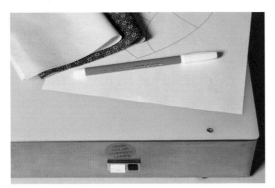

A lightbox is handy for tracing both embroidery and quilting designs onto your fabric. A glass table with a small lamp underneath or a window on a sunny day will also work. Lightboxes can be found at arts and craft stores.

CUTTING TOOLS

Good sharp scissors, both large and small, are essential. Equip yourself with the larger scissors for cutting appliqué pieces, smaller scissors for snipping threads, and a pair of utility scissors for cutting paper. A rotary cutter, see-through ruler, and cutting mat are best for squaring up blocks and cutting borders and bindings.

IRON

You will need a good steam iron. A folded white towel placed on your ironing board makes a good soft surface for pressing appliquéd designs. Always press the appliqué shapes on the wrong side.

THIMBLE

Use a thimble on your finger to push the needle when you're quilting. Although it may feel awkward at first, the thimble will soon become a part of you. There are many different styles available on the market. Try them on and find the one that fits you the best.

THREAD

For appliqué, I recommend a cotton or cotton wrapped polyester thread in a matching color. It's best to match the color of thread to the fabric in natural light for accuracy. For quilting, however, you need a thread designed specifically for quilting. You will find it comes in a rainbow of colors from which to choose. I use white all-purpose thread for basting.

EMBROIDERY FLOSS

Good quality floss gives good results. It's available in a wide array of colors so with a piece of your fabric in hand you should be able to easily find a floss that will match or coordinate in just the right shade.

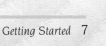

FABRICS

I use 100% cotton fabrics. My favorite for backgrounds and quilt backs is a premium quality 100% cotton, pre-shrunk, unbleached muslin with a crease-resistant finish. You will find cotton fabrics are most cooperative for appliqué, and they come in such wonderful colors and prints.

Pre-wash your fabrics if you like. I only test for colorfastness by soaking a piece of the fabric in cool water. The water will remain clear if no dye is discharged. If the water isn't clear, I rinse the entire piece of fabric before using it. Machine or air dry until it is slightly damp, then iron until completely dry.

COLORS

This technique is wide open for almost any print or color that inspires you. You may want to choose fabrics that coordinate with the appliqué shapes, the décor of a room, or maybe just a gorgeous print that catches your eye. And, of course, because you'll want to be prepared by having just what you need on hand, it's a great reason to increase that fabric stash!

For some exciting possibilities, how about crisp black and whites or the old-fashioned warmth of red on muslin? Try wild scrap bag mixes, those subtle hues of soft pastels, or the clean, bright sparkle of primary colors. Even a single color in many shades. Jump right in and add your ideas to this growing list.

BATTING

I use Poly-fil™ Traditional needle-punched batting for most of my projects. It has enough density to show dimension well, especially when closely quilted. Also it's wonderful to hand quilt, allowing the needle to glide through easily. You may want to try some small quilted samples with various battings to find your own favorite.

SPRAY STARCH

Before you begin stitching, add a couple of applications of spray starch or sizing to the background fabrics, following the manufacturer's instructions. Adding the starch or sizing makes the fabric easier to embroider without a hoop. If you prefer, of course, you may use a hoop for the projects in this book.

1 THE BACKGROUND

The cutting directions for each project will tell you to cut the background fabric at least 2" larger on all sides than the size of the background or block needed. The process of embroidery and appliqué will draw up the fabric slightly, and the extra fabric allows for this. For example, the project instructions will give you a cut size for each block, such as 10½" x 10½", and later in the directions you will trim it to the correct block size of 8½" x 8½". This block will finish at 8" after it is

pieced using a ¼" seam allowance.

Spray starch the block background and press it well. Find the center of the block background by folding it in half in both directions. Mark the center with a pin or removable marker. Use a lightbox if needed for tracing and lay the background fabric, right side up, over one copy of the pattern to be embroidered. Use the center dot to help with the placement.

Secure the fabric to the pattern with masking tape or a few pins. Then, with a removable marker, trace the entire design onto the fabric.

2 THE EMBROIDERY

Use the stem stitch, see page 11, to embroider all of the drawn lines. Add any French knots or satin stitch details if required. See page 11.

Next, remove the lines you've made with marker. If you've used a water-removable blue marker, a damp cloth will work well. If you've used a white pencil, many of the lines will rub off as you sew. You can remove any remaining lines by rubbing lightly with a damp cloth.

It's very important to allow the fabric to dry before pressing. If you press while the piece is still damp, the marker may return. Press the now-embroidered block from the back. Try not to distort or stretch the fabric as you press.

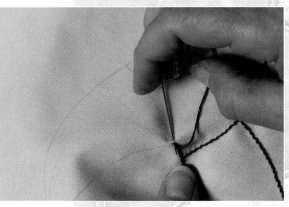

*F*or each of the projects, make two copies of your chosen design on white paper. Now that you have your supplies and fabric, you're ready to begin. Just follow these easy steps.

3 THE APPLIQUÉ

Use the second copy of your design and cut out each appliqué piece with paper scissors. These pieces will be the templates for making your appliqué shapes.

Pin each template onto the right side of the selected fabric and cut out approximately ³⁄₁₆'' from the paper's edge to add the turn-under allowance. Remove the paper template.

Next, place the appliqué shapes on the proper space formed by the embroidery, using the first copy of the paper design as a placement guide. Use one or two pins to hold in place.

Appliqué the piece, turning under the allowance as you go. Turn under the allowance far enough to have a space approximately ¹⁄₁₆''– ¹⁄₈'' between the edge of the appliqué shape and the embroidery line. The background fabric will show in this space. Try to keep the space even, but don't worry about small inconsistencies. A little bit of practice is all you need.

Fill in the spaces formed by the embroidery with an appliqué piece. There is no appliqué piece added to a few of the smaller

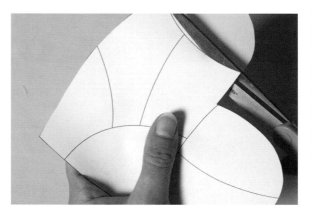

embroidered spaces such as the grass in *Fish Are A-Swimmin'*, page 38, or the stems in *Blue Ribbon Bouquet*, page 18. Press the finished block from the back.

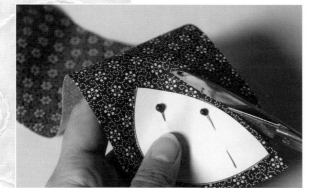

4 | ASSEMBLY

Trim the finished blocks to the sizes needed. Take care to keep the motifs centered on the blocks. Use the first copy of your pattern for reference here. Use a ¼" seam allowance to piece the blocks, sashings, and borders to form the quilt top.

Embroidery Stitches

I use two strands of floss in a color that will coordinate or complement the fabrics of each projects. The color choices are up to you, but the floss you choose should contrast with the background color. For most of the projects in the book, I've used one color of floss for all the outline embroidery. Here are tips and illustrations for the embroidery stitches you will use.

Stem Stitch

This simple stitch is used to outline the appliqués.

French Knot

This is the stitch to use if you need a raised dot or a series of them. Use it for flower centers or stamen ends. You can increase the size of the knot by using more strands of floss.

Bring the needle up from the wrong side of the fabric. Wrap the floss around the needle twice and insert the needle back into the fabric close to the thread's exit. Pull the needle through the fabric, holding the knot until all the floss is pulled through. Pull the knot but not too tightly.

Satin Stitch

This stitch works well for filling in areas where you want to have color when those spots are too small for appliqué. Use straight stitches across the shape to be filled. Keep the stitches close together.

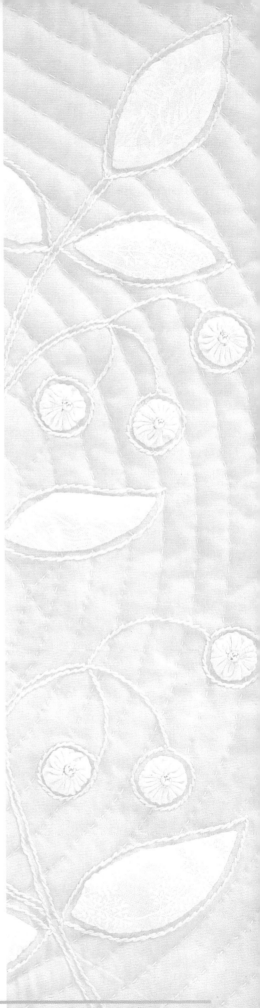

Appliqué Stitch

Thread the needle with a 12" to 18" single strand of thread in a color to match the appliqué (not the background) fabric. A longer piece of thread will wear and fray before you've used it all. Knot the end of the thread.

Keep the background fabric somewhat taut as you appliqué to avoid pushing the background fabric along with the appliqué piece. I appliqué on my lap, or I may pin the background to a small lap pillow.

Using the shaft of the needle, turn the edge of the piece under to expose the approximately 1/16" space between the appliqué and the embroidered line. Slip the knot into the fold of the turn-under by running the needle through the fold from the back of the appliqué piece and out onto the edge to be stitched down.

Insert the needle into the background, even with the thread's exit from the appliqué piece. With the needle still under the background, move the needle tip forward. Come up through the background and through a few threads on the folded edge of the appliqué piece. Pull the thread snug without drawing up the fabric.

Again, insert the needle into the background even with the thread's last exit point along the turned edge. Travel a bit under the background and come back up through the background, catching a few threads on the folded edge. Keep folding the turn-under allowance with the shaft of the needle, trimming away excess allowance if needed.

To keep your stitching consistent and comfortable, turn your work as you sew. To end, secure the thread by taking three stitches on the back behind the appliqué. Practice will make you more comfortable with the needle, fabric, and stitch.

The pieces for the appliqué designs I've used in this book are very simple. No inside points, limited curves, and all are independent of each other with no overlapping involved. They can be appliquéd in any order. You may want to number the pieces on the patterns to use as a placement reference.

Points

Once you've sewn a few points, you'll find that they are not so difficult. And they don't need to be perfect. The embroidered line keeps the eye to the point.

I try not to start stitching at a point on the appliqué shape. Once you reach a point, trim off any "ears" that appear when you turn under the allowance. Stitch up to the end of the point and take a tiny extra stitch here, then push the allowance under down the other side of the point and continue around.

Inside Curves

For inside curves, clip the seam allowance up to the turn edge as needed for a smooth turn-under execution.

Clip curve.

Circles

For more perfectly rounded circles, the key is to take one stitch at a time as you slowly turn under the allowance. If you do end up with a small point along the circumference, bring your needle out through the point and then back through the background toward the center of the circle, pulling the point inward.

Gathered Circles or Yo-Yos

For a simple-to-do circle, as well as a great design element, use a gathered circle sewn into the space outlined by embroidery. These are known as yo-yos.

Cut a circle of fabric approximately twice the size of the circle needed plus ¼'' all around. Turn under a small hem to the wrong side of the fabric and run a gathering thread around the circle through the turned under edge. Pull the thread, gathering the circle. Secure the thread with several tiny stitches on the back.

You may need to adjust the size of the circle you've cut or the hem to achieve just the size yo-yo you need. Appliqué the finished yo-yo with the gathered side up. See page 59 for an example.

BORDERS

Just as a frame shows off a painting, borders show off your lovely appliquéd blocks. You may want to add one or more borders in various widths and colors that will complement them.

Begin by measuring the sides of your appliquéd center and cut the side borders to that length. Be sure to measure after you have sewn the center together as the appliqué processes may make the center measurements less than the total of the sections before they are stitched.

Sew the side borders to the quilt and press toward the border. Then measure the top and bottom, including the side borders, and cut the borders to that measurement. Sew to the top and bottom and press. Use a ¼" seam for all borders, sashings, and block assembly. If you add a second border, repeat these steps.

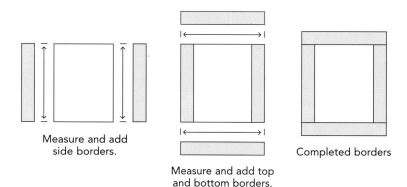

Measure and add
side borders.

Measure and add top
and bottom borders.

Completed borders

MARKING

I mark quilting lines only when necessary because I prefer to add the quilting as I go without drawing lines. For those of you who prefer marking, use a blue water-removable marker or a white fabric pencil for dark fabrics. Mark lightly, but make sure you can easily see your lines and remember to remove them before pressing.

If you are planning a quilt with a repeated quilt design and marking is necessary, see *Dresden Plate*, page 62, for more information on adding repeated designs. Before basting the layers for quilting, trace the repeated design onto the quilt top with a removable marker.

For random designs I stitch as I go without marking or mark a little at a time by pressing the tip of my needle down and dragging it across the fabric. This will leave a line for a short time, which I find works very well. Even for random designs you can use a removable marker or white pencil to mark your design before quilting if you prefer. For straight lines, masking tape works well. You'll probably find that the more hand quilting you do, the less marking you'll feel you need to add. It's just a matter of practice.

QUILTING DESIGNS

For many of my designs in this book, I began by quilting around some of the appliqué pieces on the quilt. I used a thread to match the background, and the quilting was stitched in the space between the appliqué and the embroidery. Examples of this technique are in *Rainbow Feathers*, page 50, and *Roses Are Red*, page 44. This worked as a lovely accent, but I didn't quilt around all the appliqué shapes. Next I quilted the background patterns and around the blocks.

For other quilts I quilted a random design through the background continuing into the borders. When I stitched up to an appliqué piece, the needle went between the layers and out the other side of the appliqué and back to the background. I did catch a few quilt stitches in the small spaces between the appliqué and embroidery. Examples of this type of quilting are in *Fish Are A-Swimmin,'* page 38, and *Fresh Fruit*, page 70.

Whichever technique you use, have fun with the quilting! Let your imagination loose and play with designs. Echo a shape, choose lines that represent sunlight or grasses, or stay simple with parallel lines or cross-hatching. Doodling on paper can bring surprising ideas for quilting. Look at the projects to get started and on pages 76 and 77 for more ideas.

BASTING THE LAYERS

Basting securely before you quilt will result in a smooth and flat finished piece. Cut the batting and backing at least 2" larger than the top on all sides. Lay out the backing right side down on a smooth hard surface that won't be harmed by a needle. A cutting mat is great or cardboard will also work. Add the batting and finally the quilt top with the right side up. Keeping the layers smooth and flat, use white thread to baste a grid of horizontal and vertical lines about 4" apart. Use long stitches that are approximately 1" in length. This grid basting system will secure everything in place as you quilt the designs.

QUILTING

I prefer to quilt in my lap, not a frame. I find this method most relaxing for me. With a leather thimble on my finger that pushes the needle, I stitch with a simple running stitch, taking several stitches on the needle each time as I rock both the needle and fabric.

To begin, knot a 12" to 18" length of quilting thread. A piece that is too long will fray before you use it all. Insert the needle an inch or so away from your starting point, travel under the top through the batting, and come up again at the starting point. Pull the knot through the top into the batting and begin quilting. Trust the thoroughness of the basting you've done and don't push or pull the layers as you quilt. Be sure that you're catching all three layers – the backing, batting, and quilt top. Don't hold the quilt taut; just allow it to relax as you sew.

To end a thread, knot it close to the quilt top and pull it into the batting. Let the needle travel between the layers an inch or so, then come up with the needle and snip the thread. This will leave a secure tail inside the quilt.

BINDING

Binding adds a finishing touch of color to a quilt, and in most of the projects I've selected a fabric that contrasts to the background color. I use a straight, single-fold, straight-grain binding.

To make this binding, cut 2"-wide binding strips from selvage to selvage using a rotary cutter, ruler, and mat. Sew the binding first on the sides and then the top and bottom, using a ½" seam allowance.

Turn the binding to the back and fold the raw edge under about ½". Fold the binding once more and blind stitch it down on the back, being careful not to let any stitches go through to the front. I pin the entire binding in place before stitching on the back.

And, of course, always sign and date your quilt!

ADDING BINDINGS

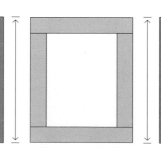

Measure and add
side bindings.

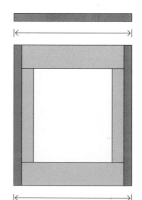

Measure and add top
and bottom bindings.

Binding ready to
turn back

BINDING CORNERS

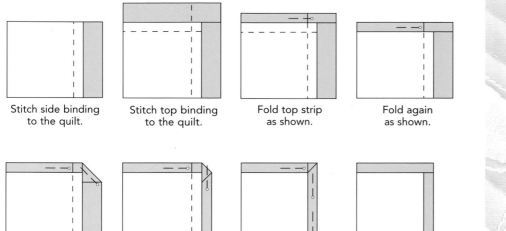

Stitch side binding
to the quilt.

Stitch top binding
to the quilt.

Fold top strip
as shown.

Fold again
as shown.

Fold side strip at
45° angle as shown.

Fold as shown.

Fold again
as shown.

Front

OTHER OPTIONS

If you like to play with fabric paints, these designs are great for stenciling. To make a stencil, just copy a design onto card stock or the dull side of freezer paper. Cut out about ³⁄₁₆" inside the drawn line. Stencil your design onto the fabric in the area where the appliqué shape would be. Allow the paint to dry and set the color according to the paint instructions. Now the embroidery lines can be sewn by hand or machine or even simply drawn with a fabric marker.

Fusible appliqué will also work very well with these designs. It can be accented with hand or machine stitching or even lines drawn with a marking pen. *Appliqué Inside the Lines* is very easy to adapt to your favorite techniques so have fun experimenting.

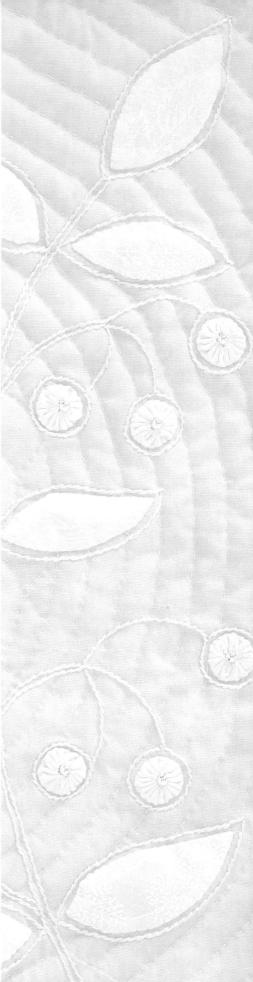

Blue Ribbon Bouquet

16½" x 22½" – finished size

True blue with a touch of yellow is a lovely color combination. Try this simple bouquet in your favorite blue shades.

MATERIALS

- Muslin for background and backing – 1 yard
- Blue fabric for border and appliqués – ¼ yard
- Yellow fabric for binding and appliqué – ¼ yard
- Assorted small pieces of blue fabrics for appliqués
- Matching thread for appliqués
- Embroidery floss – one skein of blue and one skein of yellow
- Batting – 20½" x 26½" piece
- Quilting thread – natural color

CUTTING

- From the muslin, cut one 14½" x 20½" piece for the background. Cut one 20½" x 26½" piece for the backing.
- From the blue fabric, cut two 2½" x 42" strips for the border.
- From the yellow fabric, cut three 2" x 42" strips for the binding.

DIRECTIONS

Begin by transferring the embroidery pattern onto the background fabric.

Use the stem stitch to embroider all the lines with blue floss. Embroider the flower circle centers in yellow stem stitch. Remove all marker lines and press.

From the assorted blue fabrics, appliqué the flowers, leaves, and sections of the bow, referring to the photo for color placement. From the yellow fabric, appliqué the flower centers and sections of the bow.

Press the background and trim it to 12½'' x 18½''.

Add the side, top, and bottom borders, referring to page 14. Press. When the borders have been added to the center, baste the quilt, referring to page 15.

Add the Quilting – Begin by quilting around the outside of the design right next to the embroidery. Echo quilt with ¼'' spacing two times outward around the design. Fill the bottom half of the background with randomly placed petals. Then return to the ¼'' echo lines to fill in the top areas. Quilt around the edge of the background and ¼'' out into the border on all sides.

Remove the basting and trim the batting and backing even with the quilt top. Add binding to the quilt, referring to page 16.

Block ● center

Enlarge by 143%.

Gold Pepper Berries

16¾" x 16¾" – finished size

This Hawaiian-style design is perfect for the Appliqué Inside the Lines technique. The complex pattern is simple to stitch in embroidery floss, and plenty of color abounds with the basic shapes done in appliqué.

MATERIALS

- Muslin for background and backing – ¾ yard
- Green fabric for border and appliqué – ¼ yard
- Gold fabric for binding and appliqué – ¼ yard
- Matching threads for appliqué
- Embroidery floss – two skeins of dark green
- Batting – 20¾" x 20¾" piece
- Quilting thread – natural color

CUTTING

- From the muslin, cut one 15" x 15" piece for the background. Cut one 20¾" x 20¾" piece for the backing.
- From the green fabric, cut two 2½" x 42" strips for the border.
- From the gold fabric, cut two 2" x 42" strips for the binding.

DIRECTIONS

Begin by transferring the embroidery pattern onto the background fabric.

Use the stem stitch to embroider the solid lines with dark green floss. Remove all marker lines and press.

From the green fabrics, appliqué the leaves and from the gold fabric, appliqué the berries. The appliqué shapes are marked with dotted lines on the pattern.

Press the background and trim it to 13" x 13".

Add the side, top, and bottom borders, referring to page 14. Press. When the borders have been added to the center, baste the quilt, referring to page 15.

Add the Quilting – Quilt just outside the embroidery all around the design. Stitch outside the stem-stitched square in the center. Quilt in-the-ditch around the block and ¼" inside the block. Quilt ¼" outside the block in the border.

Remove the basting and trim the batting and backing even with the quilt top. Add binding to the quilt, referring to page 16.

Flip and trace on dashed lines.

Block center

Golden Stars

18½" x 25½" – finished size

The added sparkle of metallic gold brightens the mixed pastel stars in this six-block quilt. For a finishing touch, add a favorite button to the center of each star. Perfect for that special little girl's room!

MATERIALS

- Muslin for background and backing – 1¼ yards
- Pink fabric for border – ¼ yard
- Yellow fabric for binding – ¼ yard
- Assorted small pieces of pastel fabric for appliqué – pinks, yellows, blues
- Matching threads for appliqués
- Embroidery floss – one skein of metallic gold
- Batting – 22½" x 29½" piece
- Quilting thread – natural color
- Six buttons – approximately ¾" in diameter

CUTTING

- From the muslin, cut six 9½" x 9½" blocks. Cut one 22½" x 29½" piece for the backing.
- From the pink fabric, cut three 2½" x 42" strips for the border.
- From the yellow fabric, cut three 2" x 42" strips for the binding.

DIRECTIONS

Begin by transferring the embroidery pattern onto the blocks.

Use the stem stitch to embroider all the lines with gold metallic floss. Use short lengths of this floss as it wears more quickly than cotton and longer pieces will become frayed. Remove all the marker lines and press.

From the assorted pastel fabrics, appliqué the star points. See the photo for color placement.

Press the blocks and trim them to 7½" x 7½".

Sew the six blocks together in three rows with two blocks in each row. Sew the rows together to make the quilt center.

Add the side, top, and bottom borders, referring to page 14. Press. When the borders have been added to the center, baste the quilt, referring to page 15.

Add the Quilting – Use simple quilting to accent these simple stars. Begin by quilting around the appliqué pieces and in-the-ditch around the blocks. Quilt ¼" outside each star, ¼" inside each block, and ¼" outside the blocks in the border.

Remove the basting and trim the batting and backing even with the quilt top. Add binding to the quilt, referring to page 16. Stitching through all layers, sew a button in the center of each star.

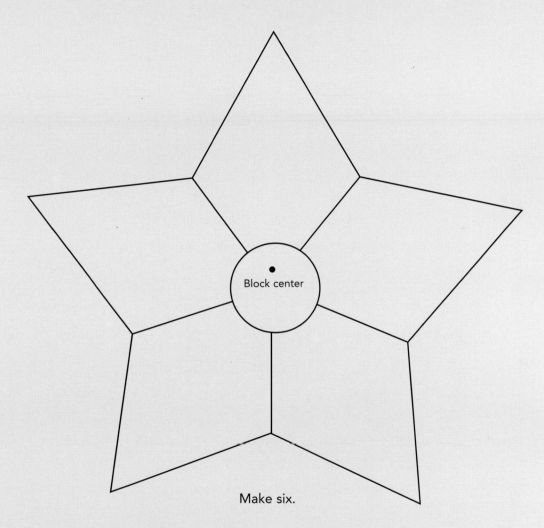

Block center

Make six.

Six in Bloom

19½" x 27½" – finished size

MATERIALS

- Muslin for blocks and backing – 1⅓ yards
- Green fabric for border – ¼ yard
- Red fabric for binding – ¼ yard
- Assorted small pieces of red, yellow, purple, green, and blue fabric for appliqués
- Matching threads for appliqués
- Embroidery floss – two skeins of medium green and one skein of yellow
- Batting – 23½" x 31½" piece
- Quilting thread – natural color

CUTTING

- From the muslin fabric, cut six 10½" x 10½" blocks. Cut one 23½" x 31½" piece for the backing.
- From the green fabric, cut three 2" x 42" strips for the border.
- From the red fabric, cut four 2" x 42" strips for the binding.

This delightful garden is all in bloom with six different blossoms for embroidery and appliqué. Simple-to-appliqué shapes come together to form these graceful flowers.

DIRECTIONS

Begin by transferring the embroidery patterns onto the blocks.

Use the stem stitch to embroider the flower, stem, and leaf outlines with medium green floss. Use short straight green stitches in the bases of the flowers as shown on the patterns. For the flower stamens, stitch with yellow embroidery floss, using the stem stitch and French knots. Remove all marker lines and press.

From the assorted red, yellow, purple, green, and blue fabrics, appliqué the petal and leaf pieces. See the photo for placement.

Press the blocks and trim each to 8½" x 8½".

Sew the six blocks together in three rows with two blocks in each row. Refer to the photo for arrangement of the flower blocks or place them in a pleasing arrangement of your own.

Add the side, top, and bottom borders, referring to page 14. Press. When the borders have been added to the center, baste the quilt, referring to page 15.

Add the Quilting – Stitch an allover quilting pattern for this quilt. Begin quilting random shells in the lower left corner and continue outward through the quilt center and borders.

Remove the basting and trim the batting and backing even with the quilt top. Add binding to the quilt, referring to page 16.

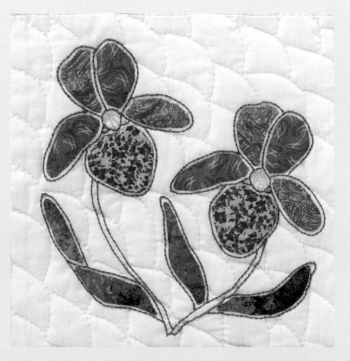

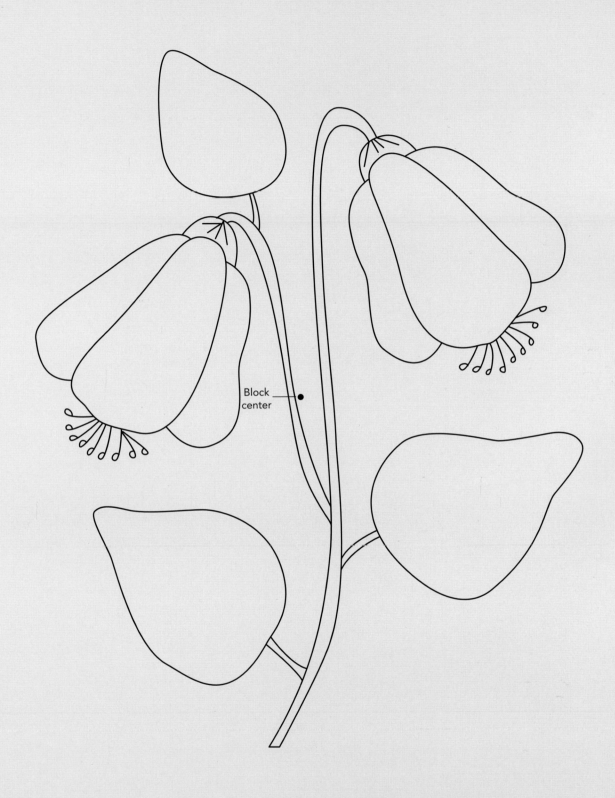

Block
center

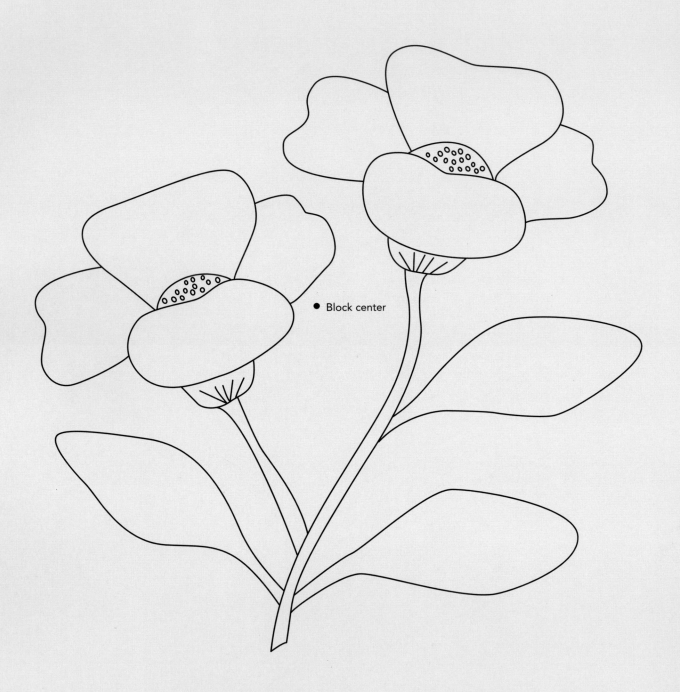

● Block center

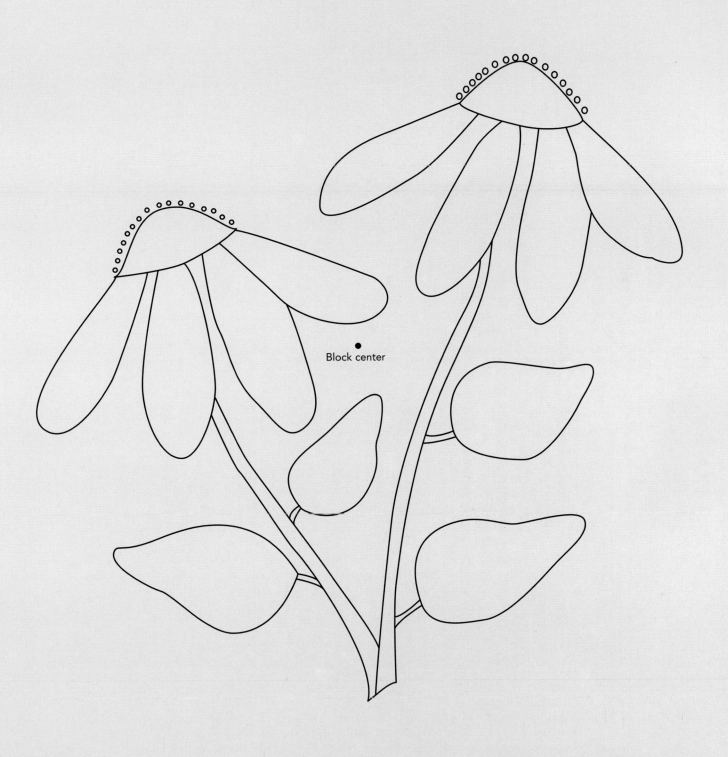

Block center

● Block center

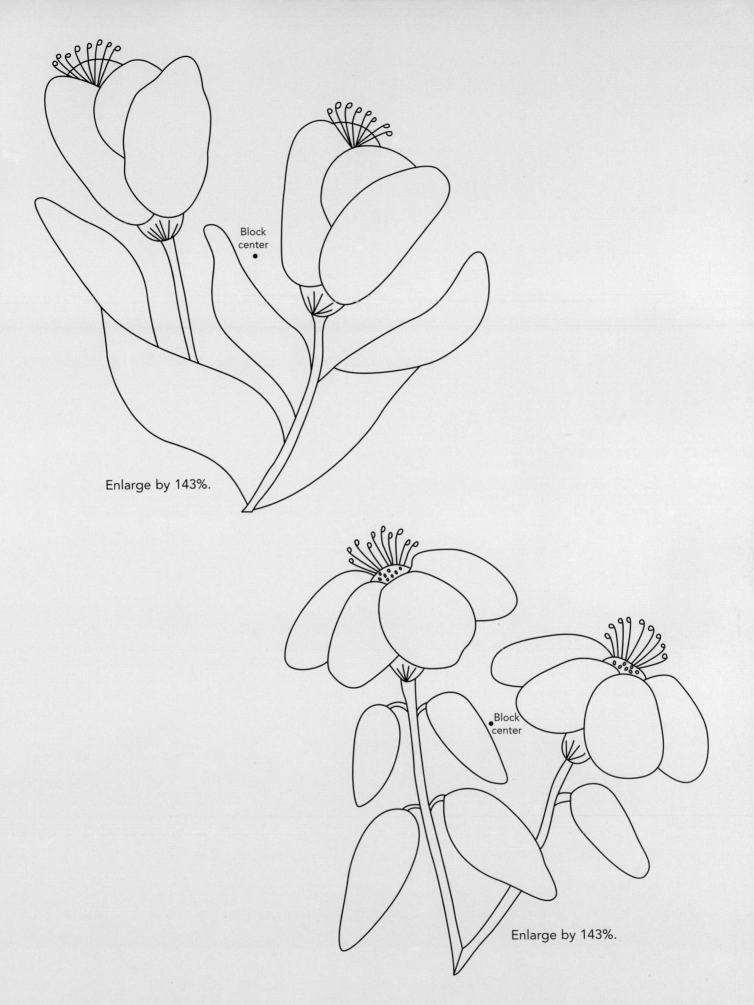

Block
center

Enlarge by 143%.

Block
center

Enlarge by 143%.

The summertime greens of a small pond are reflected in these lazy fish. Close your eyes and you can almost feel the warmth of a late August day.

Fish Are A-Swimmin'

19½" x 27½" – finished size

MATERIALS

- Muslin for blocks and backing –1¼ yards
- Blue fabric for border – ¼ yard
- Green fabric for binding – ¼ yard
- Assorted small pieces of blue, green, brown, and cream fabric for appliqués
- Matching thread for appliqués
- Embroidery floss - two skeins of medium green
- Batting – 23½" x 31½"
- Quilting thread – natural color

CUTTING

- From the muslin, cut three 10½" x 18½" blocks. Cut one 23½" x 31½" piece for the backing.
- From the blue fabric, cut three 2" x 42" strips for the border.
- From the green fabric, cut four 2" x 42" strips for the binding.

DIRECTIONS

Begin by transferring the embroidery patterns onto the blocks.

Use the stem stitch to embroider the fish and plant lines with medium green floss. Remove the marker lines and press.

From the assorted blue, green, brown, and cream fabrics, appliqué the fish and rounded leaf pieces.

Press the blocks and trim them to 8½" x 16½".

Sew the three blocks together referring to the photo for placement.

Add the side, top, and bottom borders, referring to page 14. Press. When the borders have been added to the center, baste the quilt, referring to page 15.

Add the Quilting – Quilt irregular wavy lines running up and down in an overall pattern. Mark the lines as you sew using a removable marker or quilt without marking if you prefer. Continue the quilting into the border.

Remove the basting and trim the batting and backing even with the quilt top. Add binding to the quilt, referring to page 16.

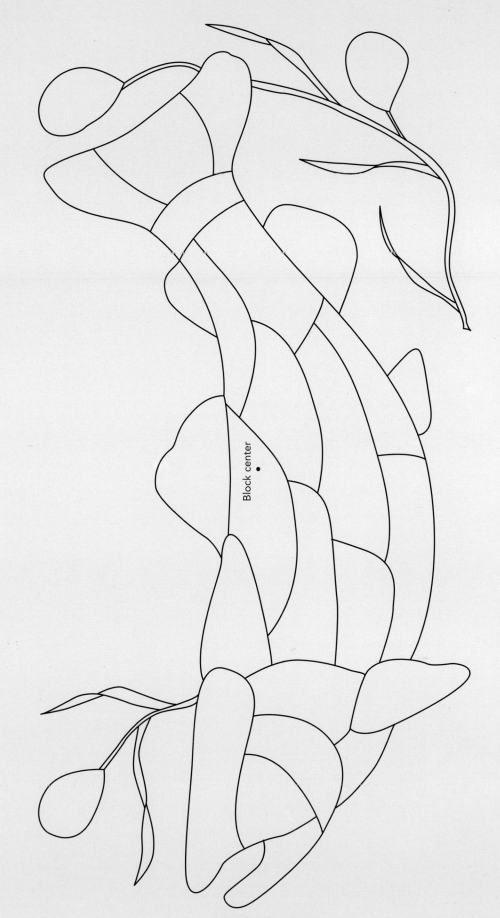

Block center

Enlarge by 167%.

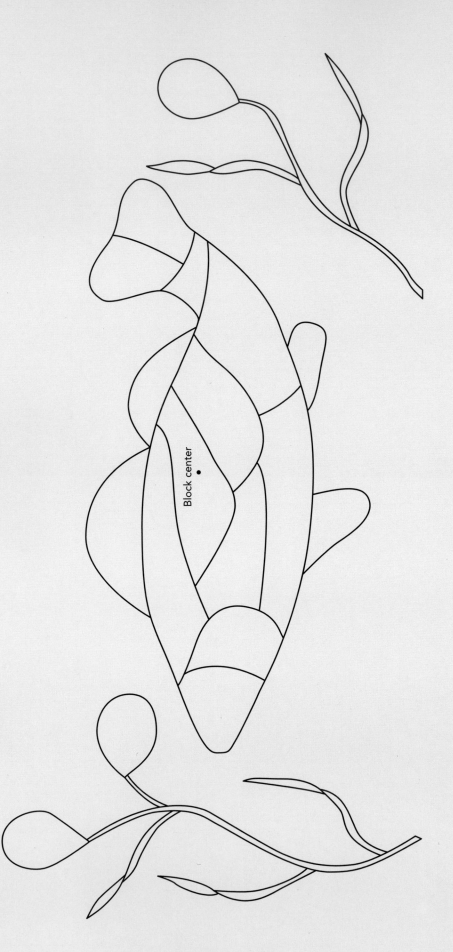

Block center

Enlarge by 167%.

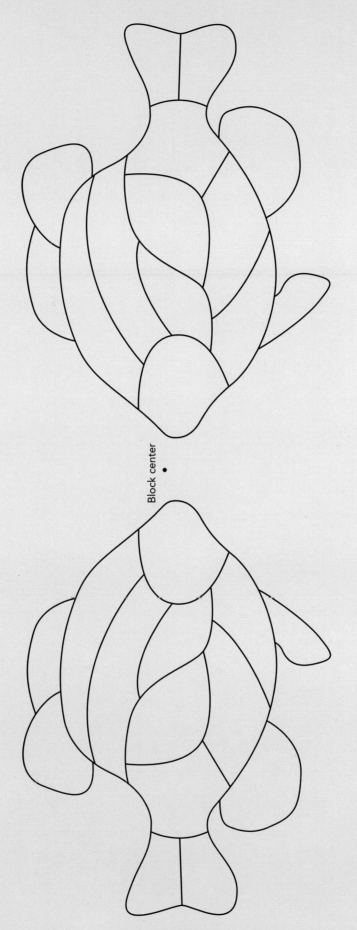

Block center

Enlarge by 167%.

Roses Are Red

26½" x 26½" – finished size

Yes, roses are red and hearts are too. Add a pair of birds and a center sun for a bright and cheery quilt with a new twist on simple and traditional redwork embroidery.

MATERIALS

- Muslin for blocks and backing -1¾ yards
- Assorted red prints for appliqués, borders, and binding – ¼ yard each of eight fabrics
- Matching thread for appliqués
- Embroidery floss – two skeins of red
- Batting – 30½" x 30½" piece
- Quilting thread – natural color

CUTTING

- From the muslin, cut nine 9½" x 9½" blocks. Cut one 30½" x 30½" piece for the backing.
- From the assorted red prints, cut one 3" x 42" strip from four different prints for the border. Cut four 2" x 42" strips from one red print for the binding.

DIRECTIONS

Begin by transferring the embroidery patterns onto the blocks. There is one sun block, four heart blocks, one bird block as shown on the pattern and one reversed, and one rose block as shown on the pattern and one reversed.

Use the stem stitch to embroider the lines with red embroidery floss. Remove the marker lines and press.

From the assorted red prints, appliqué the pieces for each design.

Press the blocks and trim to 7½'' x 7½''.

Sew the nine blocks together in three rows with three blocks in each row. Sew the rows together, referring to the photo for placement.

Use a different red print for each side of the quilt and add the side, top, and bottom borders, referring to page 14. When the borders have been added to the center, baste the quilt, referring to page 15.

Add the Quilting – Begin by quilting a line from corner to corner in each direction. Echo quilt down each triangle formed, using 1'' masking tape and continuing the quilting into the border. Quilt around some of the appliqué shapes.

Remove the basting and trim the batting and backing even with the quilt top. Add binding to the quilt, referring to page 16.

Block center

Make one and make one reversed.

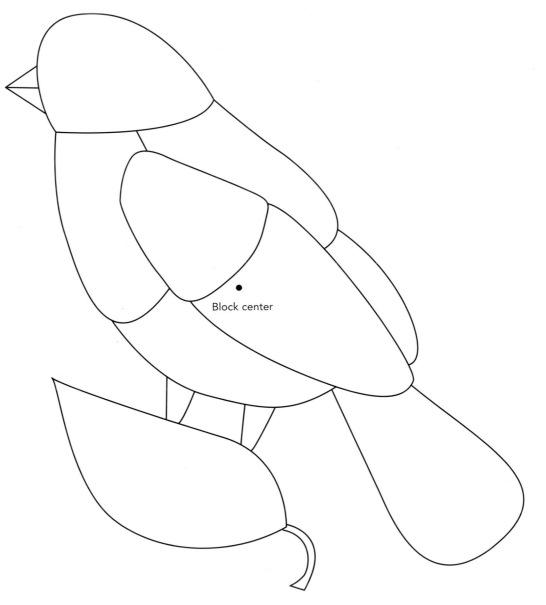

Block center

Make one and make one reversed.

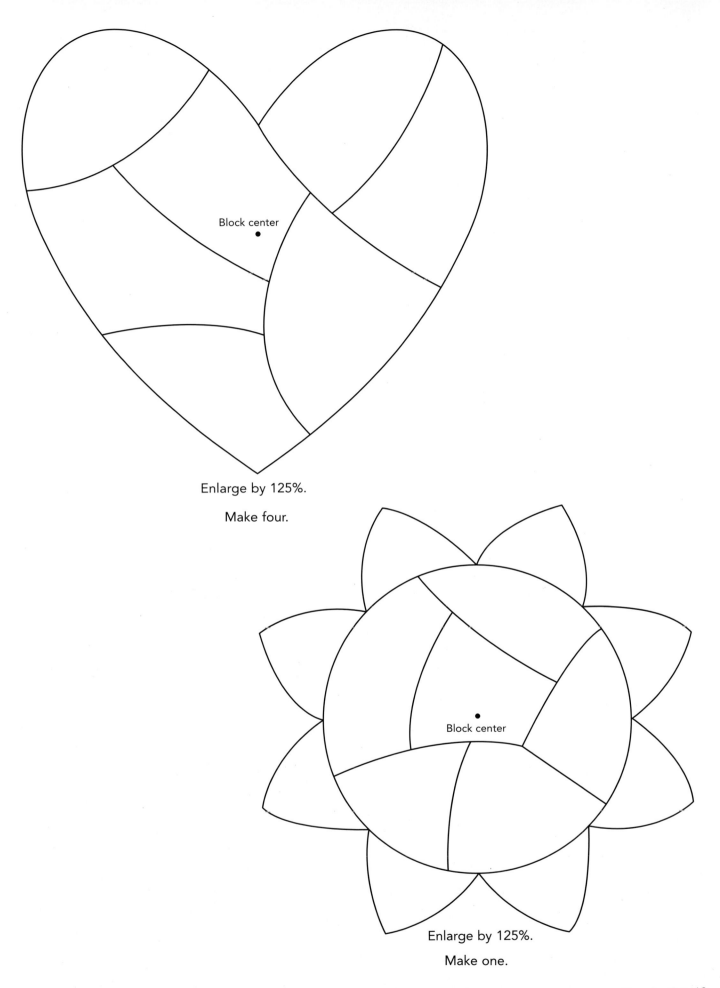

Block center

Enlarge by 125%.

Make four.

Block center

Enlarge by 125%.

Make one.

Rainbow Feathers

27½" x 15½" – finished size

These feathers are often seen as quilting motifs, but add a little color and the results are spectacular. I collected scraps of reds to yellows for the first feather, greens for the second feather, and blues to purples for the third feather.

MATERIALS

- Muslin for blocks and backing -1 yard
- Black fabric for binding, border, and sashing -½ yard
- Assorted small pieces of red, yellow, green, blue, and purple fabric for appliqués
- Matching threads for appliqués
- Embroidery floss – one skein of black
- Batting – 31½" x 19½" piece
- Quilting thread – natural color

CUTTING

- From the muslin, cut three 9½" x 13½" blocks. Cut one 31½" x 19½" piece for the backing.
- From the black fabric, cut two 1½" x 11½" pieces for the sashing. Cut three 2½" x 42" strips for the border. Cut three 2" x 42" strips for the binding.

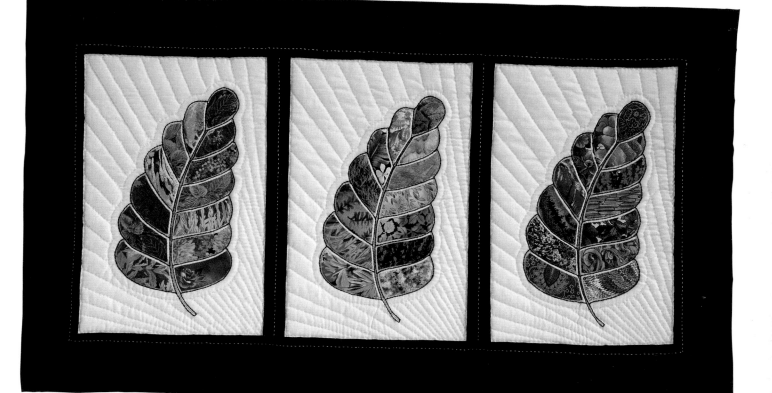

DIRECTIONS

Begin by transferring the embroidery pattern onto the blocks.

Use the stem stitch to embroider the feathers with black floss. Remove the marker lines and press.

From the assorted red and yellow fabrics, appliqué the first feather. Appliqué the second feather with the green fabrics and the third with the blue and purple fabrics.

Press the blocks and trim them to 7½" x 11½".

Assemble the quilt center by sewing the two sashing pieces between the three feather blocks.

Add the side, top, and bottom borders, referring to page 14. Press. When the borders have been added to the center, baste the quilt, referring to page 15.

Add the Quilting – Begin by quilting around each feather. Echo quilt ¼" out from the stitching line. Stitch in-the-ditch around each block. Radiate lines from the lower right corner of each block to the upper left as shown in the photo. Add quilting through the middle of each sashing strip and around the inside edge of the border approximately ¼" from the edge.

Remove the basting and trim the batting and backing even with the quilt top. Add binding to the quilt, referring to page 16.

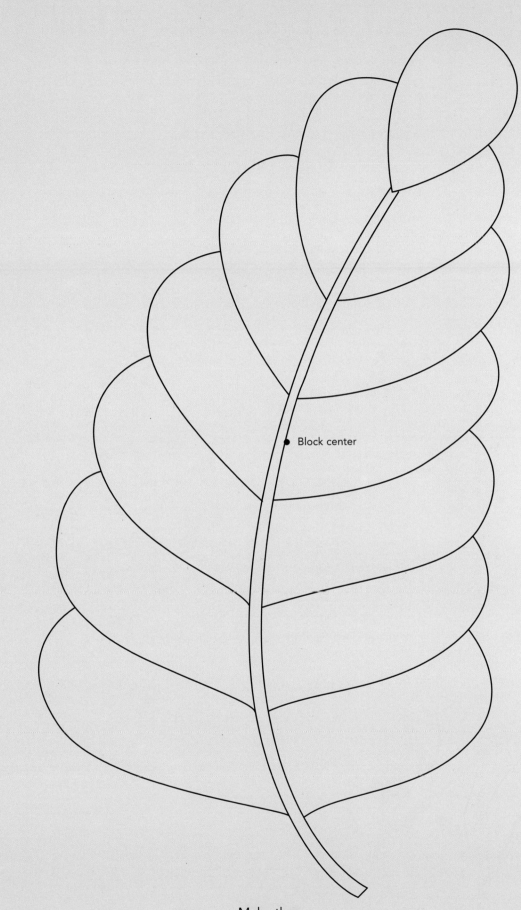

Block center

Make three.

Basic Black and White

11" x 28½" – finished size

The impact of black and white is even more dramatic when it is combined with these geometric lines and angles. For a finishing touch — a collection of modern-looking buttons.

MATERIALS

- Black fabric for blocks and binding – ½ yard
- White-on-white print fabric for border and sashing – ⅜ yard
- Assorted small pieces of white-on-white prints for appliqués
- Muslin for backing – ½ yard
- White thread for appliqués
- Embroidery floss – one skein of white
- Batting – 15" x 32½" piece
- Quilting thread – black and white
- Twenty-two assorted buttons – black and white

CUTTING

- From the black fabric, cut three 10" x 10" blocks. Cut three 2" x 42" strips for the binding.
- From the white-on-white print, cut two 1¼" x 8" pieces for the sashing. Cut three 2" x 42" strips for the border.
- From the muslin, cut one 15" x 32½" piece for the backing.

DIRECTIONS

Begin by transferring the embroidery patterns onto the blocks.

Use the stem stitch to embroider all the lines with white floss. Remove the marker lines and press.

From the assorted white-on-white prints, appliqué the shapes inside the embroidery.

Press the blocks and trim them to 8'' x 8''.

Sew the three blocks together with the two sashing strips between them, referring to the photo for placement.

Add the side, top, and bottom borders, referring to page 14. Press. When the borders have been added to the center, baste the quilt, referring to page 15.

Add the Quilting – Quilt around some or all of the applique pieces in black. The black thread will not add any confusing lines among the embroidery. With the white quilting thread, quilt ¼'' inside the black blocks and in-the-ditch around the outside of the blocks.

Remove the basting and trim the batting and backing even with the quilt top. Add binding to the quilt, referring to page 16. Stitching through all layers, sew a button in the center of each appliqué shape as shown in the photo.

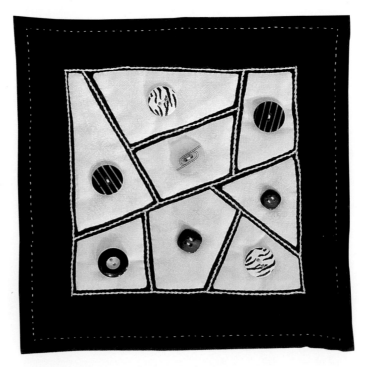

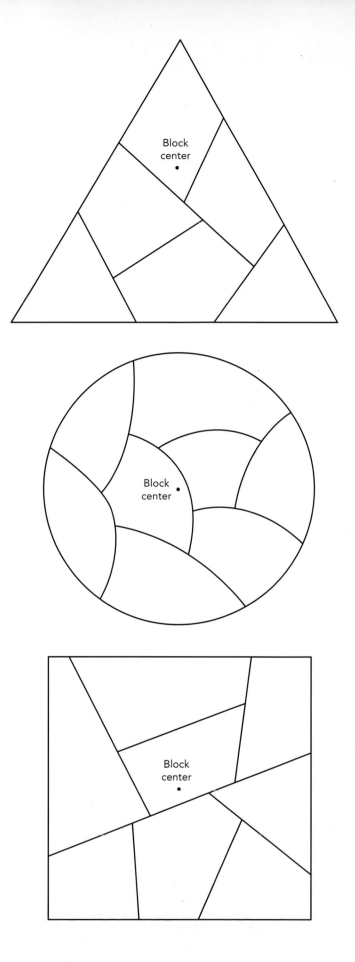

Block
center

Block
center

Block
center

Enlarge by 200%.

Vanilla Leaves

17½" x 17½" – finished size

A swirl of circular quilting adds the unique finishing touch to this simply elegant quilt in shades of cream and pastel green, or choose your own favorite soft color for the background.

MATERIALS

- Pastel green fabric for background and binding - ½ yard
- Green print for sashing and border – ¼ yard
- Assorted cream print fabrics for appliqués
- Muslin for backing – ⅔ yard
- Cream thread for appliqués
- Embroidery floss – one skein of cream
- Batting – 21½" x 21½" piece
- Quilting thread – natural color
- Twelve silver beads – about 3mm (optional)

CUTTING

- From the pastel green fabric, cut one 8½" x 15½" block. Cut two 8½" x 8½" blocks. Cut two 2" x 42" strips for the binding.
- From the green print fabric, cut one 1½" x 6½" piece and one 1½" x 13½" piece for sashing. Cut two 2½" x 42" strips for borders.
- From the assorted cream print fabrics, cut twelve circles 1¾" in diameter for the berries.
- From the muslin, cut one 21½" x 21½" piece for the backing.

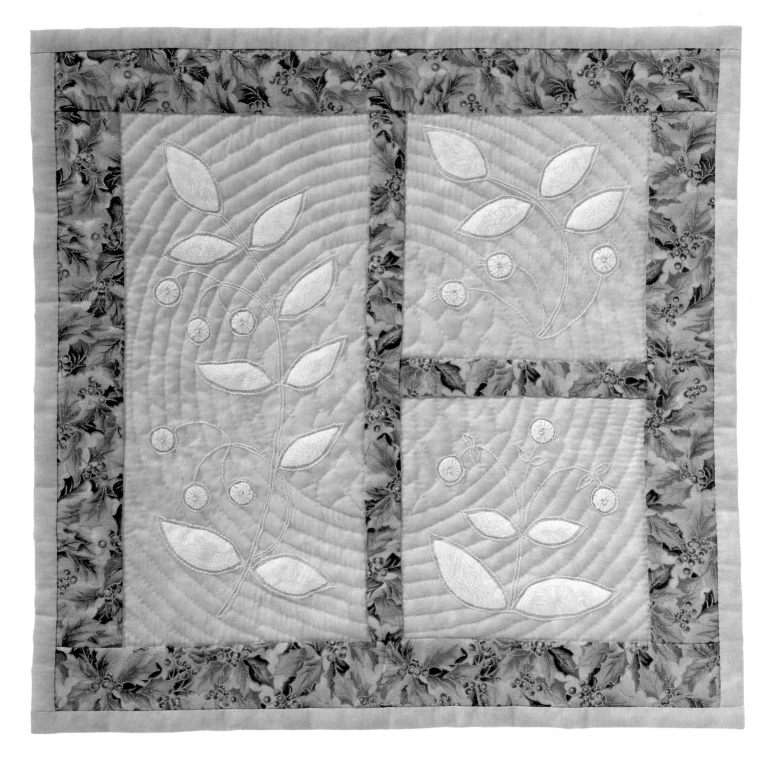

DIRECTIONS

Begin by transferring the embroidery patterns onto the blocks.

Use the stem stitch to embroider all the lines with cream floss. Remove the marker lines and press.

From the assorted cream print fabrics, appliqué the large leaves. Make yo-yos for the berries, referring to page 13. Appliqué the yo-yos in place.

Trim the larger block to 6½'' x 13½''. Trim the two smaller blocks to 6½'' x 6½''.

Sew the shorter sashing piece between the two smaller blocks as shown in the photo. Press.

Sew the longer sashing piece to the right side of the larger block. Press. Sew the two sections together as shown in the photo.

Add the side, top, and bottom borders, referring to page 14. Press. When the borders have been added to the center, baste the quilt, referring to page 15.

Add the Quilting – Begin by quilting a circle in the center of the quilt. I used a saucer to create a circle that was approximately 6 ½''in diameter. Fill the inside of the circle with random shells. Quilt the background fabric only, not sashings, appliqué, or borders. Echo the circle outward in lines about ⅜'' apart. Stop at the border. Quilt in-the-ditch around each block.

Remove the basting and trim the batting and backing even with the quilt top. Add binding to the quilt, referring to page 16. Sewing through all layers of the quilt, stitch the beads to the centers of the yo-yos.

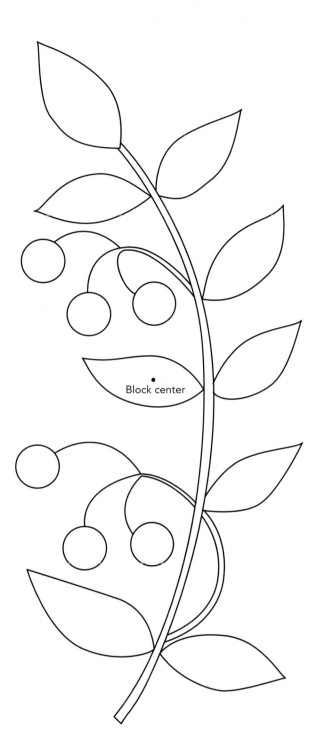

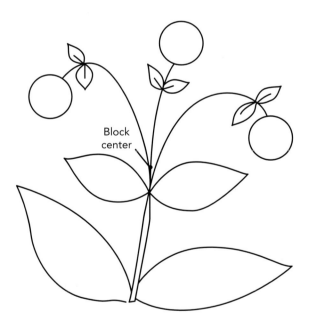

Block center

Block center

Block center

Block center

Enlarge by 167%.

Dresden Plate

15½" x 15½"– finished size

This traditionally-pieced block is stunning when embroidered and appliquéd in an array of lovely jewel tones. This single block is a great beginner's project.

MATERIALS

- Muslin for background and backing – ⅔ yard
- Assorted prints or four ⅛ yard pieces of fabric for the border
- Assorted prints or four ⅛ yard pieces of fabric for the binding
- Assorted print fabric pieces for appliqués
- Matching threads for appliqués
- Embroidery floss – one skein of medium green
- Batting –19½" x 19½" piece
- Quilting thread – natural color

CUTTING

- From the muslin, cut one 13½" x 13½" piece for the background. Cut one 19½" x 19½" piece for the backing.

- From the assorted prints, cut two 2½" x 11½" pieces for the side borders Cut two 2½" x 15½" pieces for the top and bottom borders and four 2" x 20" strips for the binding. Cut one 2" circle for yo-yo center.

DIRECTIONS

Begin by transferring the embroidery pattern onto the background fabric.

Use the stem stitch to embroider all the lines with medium green floss. Remove the marker lines and press.

From the assorted prints, appliqué the large sections of the plate. Make a yo-yo for the center circle referring to page 13 for instructions. Appliqué in place.

Press the background and trim to 11½" x 11½".

Add the side, top, and bottom borders, referring to page 14. Press. When the borders have been added to the center, baste the quilt, referring to page 15.

Add the Quilting – Quilt around the appliqué pieces and echo quilt ¼" out from the plate. Stitch the marked corner designs and around the block. Quilt in the border ¼" from the seam line.

Remove the basting and trim the batting and backing even with the quilt top. Add binding to the quilt, referring to page 16.

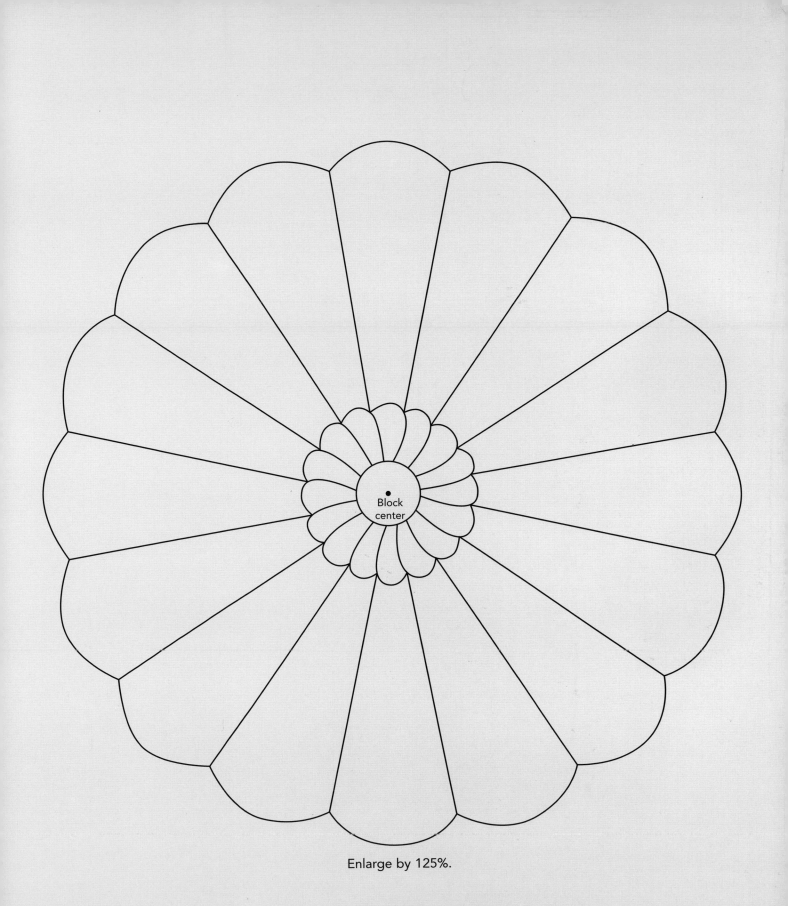

Block
center

Enlarge by 125%.

Floral Butterflies

8" x 8" and 7" x 7" – finished sizes

These little projects are a great place to jump in and try this embroidery and appliqué technique. Think even bigger and imagine a bed covered in beautiful butterflies. Start collecting those floral fabrics!

MATERIALS

- Muslin for backgrounds and backing – ½ yard
- Assorted small print pieces for borders and appliqués
- Matching threads for appliqués
- Embroidery floss – one skein of black
- Batting – two 8½" x 8½" pieces and one 7½" x 7½" piece
- Quilting thread – natural color

CUTTING

Large Butterfly

From the muslin, cut one 8½" x 8½" piece for the background and one 8½" x 8½" piece for the backing. From the assorted prints, cut one 1½" x 42" strip for the border.

Small Butterfly

From the muslin, cut one 6½'' x 6½'' piece for the background and one 7½'' x 7½'' piece for the backing. From the assorted prints, cut one 2'' x 42'' strip for the border.

Two Small Butterflies

From the muslin, cut one 8½'' x 8½'' piece for the background and one 8½'' x 8½'' piece for the backing. From the assorted prints, cut one 1½'' x 42'' strip for the border.

DIRECTIONS

Begin by transferring the embroidery patterns onto the blocks.

Use the stem stitch to embroider all the lines with black floss. Use several short straight stitches together for the end of the antennae. Remove the marker lines and press.

From the assorted prints, appliqué the wing pieces.

Trim the two larger blocks to 6½" x 6½" and the smaller block to 4½" x 4½".

Add the side, top, and bottom borders, referring to page 14. Press.

With right sides up, lay the appliquéd blocks on top of the batting pieces. Lay the backing pieces on top with the right side down. Using a ¼" seam, sew around the blocks, leaving at least a 2½" unstitched opening on one side for turning. Trim the corner seam allowances and turn right side out. Press. Blindstitch the opening closed.

Add the Quilting – Add simple quilting to these simple little quilts. Quilt around the butterflies and the border in the background fabric.

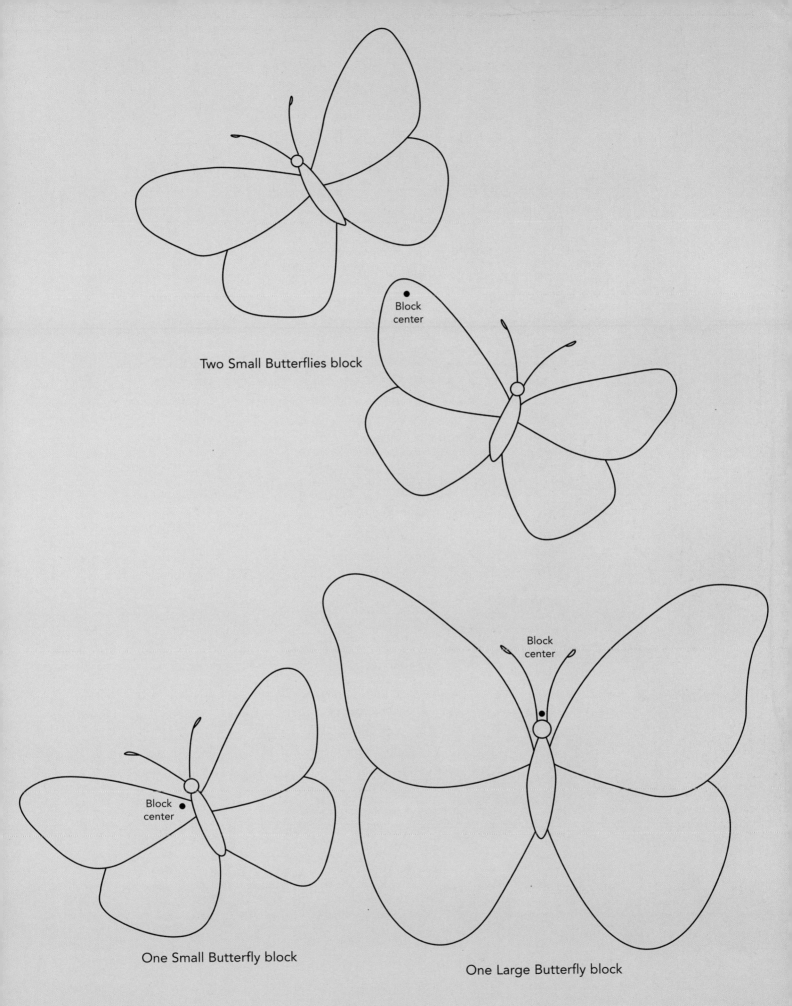

Two Small Butterflies block

Block
center

Block
center

Block
center

One Small Butterfly block

One Large Butterfly block

Fresh Fruit

20½" x 28½" – finished size

Luscious fruit colors combine with your favorite greens to create this six-block quilt. A delightful accent for the breakfast nook!

MATERIALS

- Muslin for blocks and backing -1⅓ yards
- Green print fabric for border – ¼ yard
- Green fabric for binding -¼ yard
- Assorted small pieces of red, yellow, peach, purple, and green fabric for appliqués
- Matching threads for appliqués
- Embroidery floss – two skeins of green
- Batting – 24½" x 32½" piece
- Quilting thread – natural color

CUTTING

- From the muslin, cut six 10½" x 10½" blocks. Cut one 24½" x 30½" piece for the backing.
- From the green print fabric, cut three 2½" x 42" strips for the border. Cut four 2" x 42" strips for the binding.

DIRECTIONS

Begin by transferring the embroidery patterns onto the blocks.

Use the stem stitch to embroider all the lines with green floss. Use a few short straight stitches for the bottom of the apples. See the color photo for placement. Remove all marker lines and press.

From the assorted fruit-colored fabrics, appliqué the fruit. Appliqué the leaves from green fabric.

Press the blocks and trim to 8½'' x 8½''.

Sew the six blocks together in three rows with two blocks in each row. Sew the rows together to make the quilt top. Refer to the color photo for placement of the fruit blocks, or place them in a pleasing arrangement of your own.

Add the side, top, and bottom borders, referring to page 14. Press. When the borders have been added to the center, baste the quilt, referring to page 15.

Add the Quilting – Stitch an overall pattern on this quilt. Begin by stitching arched lines with large spaces between them. Then fill in these spaces by echoing the main lines with lines that are approximately ¼'' apart. Continue the quilting into the border.

Remove the basting and trim the batting and backing even with the quilt top. Add binding to the quilt, referring to page 16.

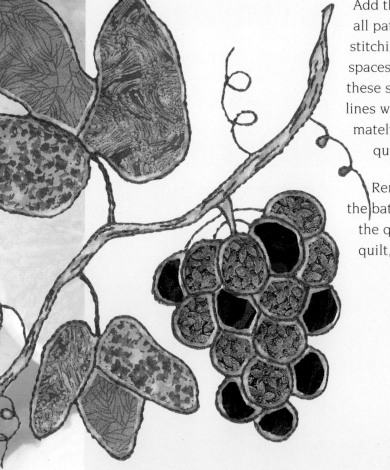

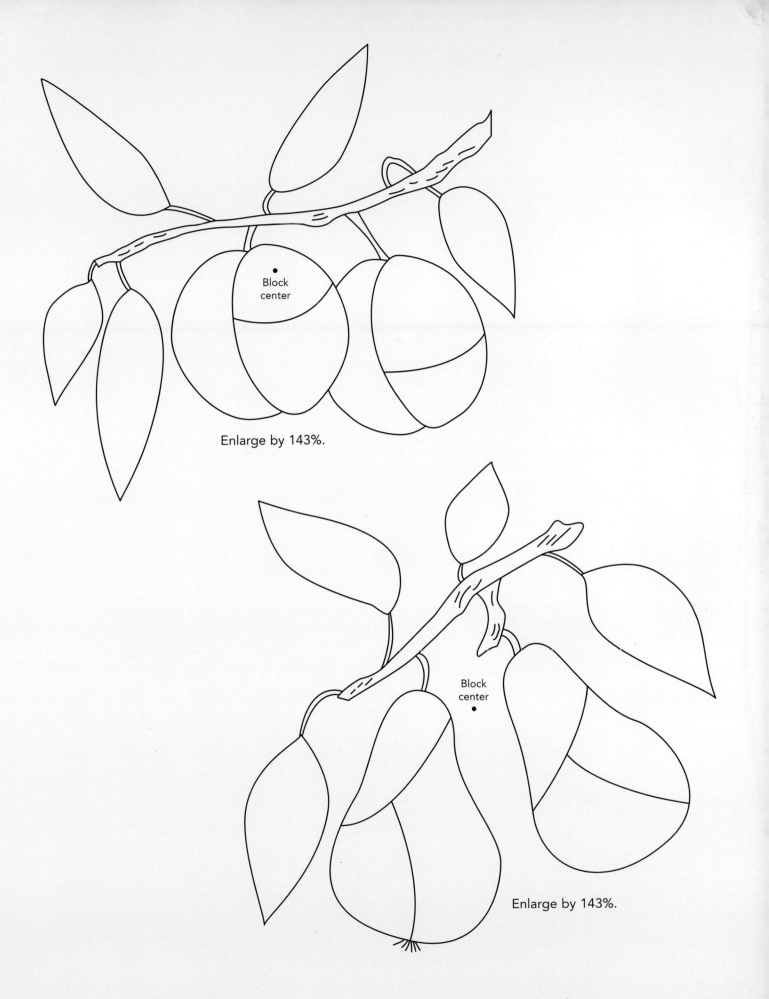

Block
center

Enlarge by 143%.

Block
center

Enlarge by 143%.

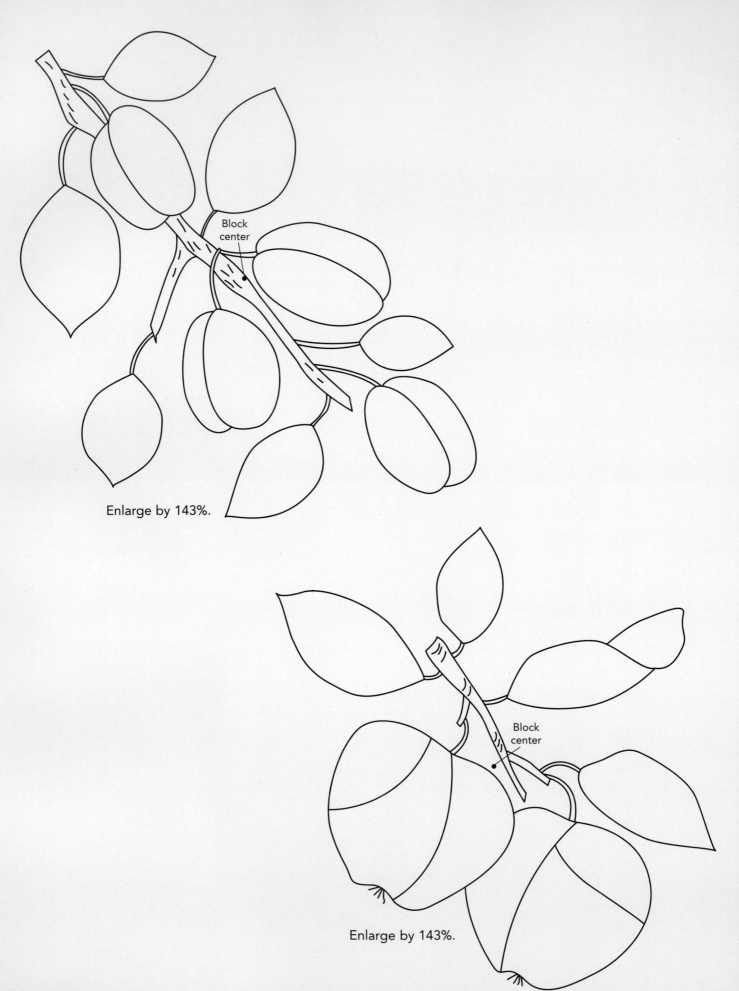

Block
center

Enlarge by 143%.

Block
center

Enlarge by 143%.

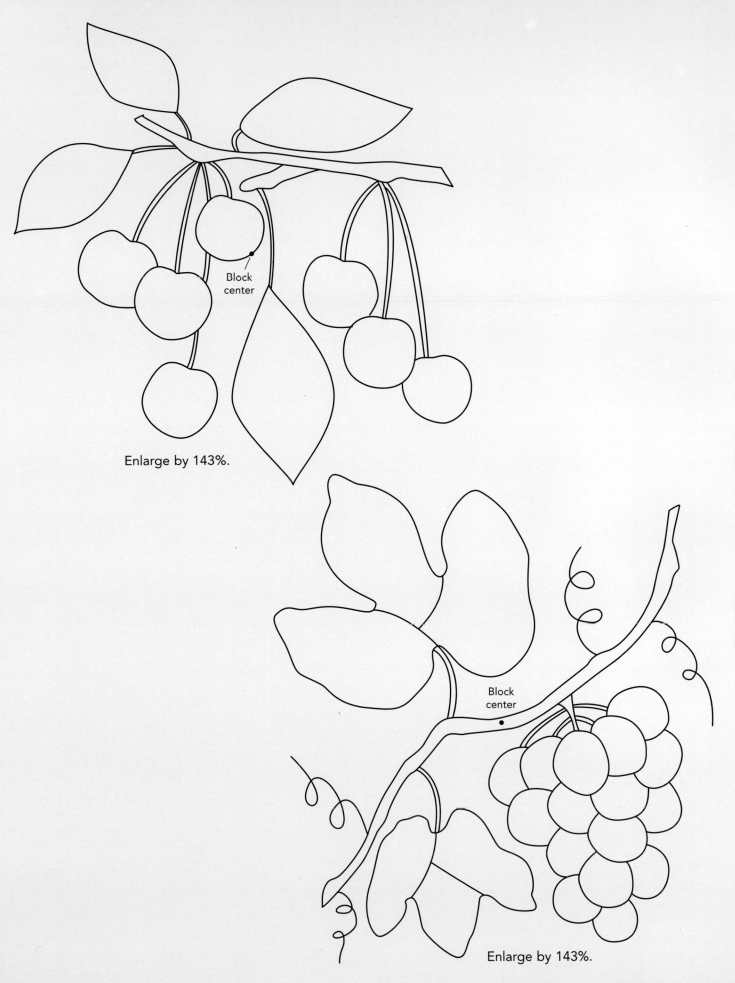

Block
center

Enlarge by 143%.

Block
center

Enlarge by 143%.

About the Author

In *Appliqué Inside the Lines*, Carol Armstrong has again used her own unique and artistic style to create a fresh, new look for traditional

appliqué. As in her other favorite books, she gathers her inspiration from the natural surroundings of her Michigan home or from any other subject that may catch her artistic eye.

She says the wonderfully snowy winters in Michigan's Upper Peninsula where she lives with her cabinetmaker husband give her lots of time for quilting. Together they enjoy their creative, homestead life-style. When her fingers and eyes need a break, there is always water to pump and bring to the house, wood to load into the wood box, bird feeders to fill, or the large organic vegetable garden to tend in the summers.

Index

A
Appliqué 10
Appliqué stitch 12
Author biography 78

B
Background 9
Basic Black and White 54
Basting 15
Batting 8
Between needles 6
Binding 16
Blue marker 6
Blue Ribbon Bouquet 18
Borders 14

C
Circles 13
Colors 8
Cotton thread 7
Cotton wrapped
    polyester thread 7
Cutting mat 7
Cutting tools 7

D
Dresden Plate 62

E
Embroidery 9
Embroidery floss 7, 11
Embroidery hoop 8
Embroidery needles 6
Embroidery stitches 11

F
Fabric paints 17
Fabric pencils 6
Fabrics 8
Finishing 14
Fish Are A-Swimmin' 38
Floral Butterflies 66
French knot 11
Fresh Fruit 70
Fusible appliqué 17

G
Gathered circles 13
Glass-headed pins 6
Gold Pepper Berries 22
Golden Stars 26

I
Inside curves 13
Iron 7

L
Lightbox 7

M
Marking 14
Marking tools 6
Milliners' needles 6
Muslin 8

P
Pins 6
Points 13
Pre-wash 8

Q
Quilting 15
Quilting designs 15, 76, 77

R
Rainbow Feathers 50
Roses Are Red 44
Rotary cutter 7
Running stitch 15

S
Satin stitch 11
Scissors 7
Seam allowance 11
Sharps needles 6
Silk pins 6
Six in Bloom 30
Spray starch 8
Stem stitch 11
Stenciling 17
Supplies 6

T
Techniques 9
Templates 10
Thimble 7
Thread 7

V
Vanilla Leaves 58

Y
Yo-Yos 13

15 Two-Block Quilts: Unlock the Secrets of Secondary Patterns, Claudia Olson

250 Continuous-Line Quilting Designs for Hand, Machine & Long-Arm Quilters, Laura Lee Fritz

250 More Continuous-Line Quilting Designs for Hand, Machine & Long-Arm Quilters, Laura Lee Fritz

All About Quilting from A to Z, From the Editors and Contributors of Quilter's Newsletter Magazine and Quiltmaker Magazine

America from the Heart: Quilters Remember September 11, 2001, Karey Bresenhan

An Amish Adventure, 2nd Edition: A Workbook for Color in Quilts, Roberta Horton

Appliqué 12 Easy Ways!: Charming Quilts, Giftable Projects, & Timeless Techniques, Elly Sienkiewicz

Appliqué Inside the Lines: 12 Quilt Projects to Embroider & Appliqué, Carol Armstrong

Art of Classic Quiltmaking, The, Harriet Hargrave & Sharyn Craig

Art of Machine Piecing, The: How to Achieve Quality Workmanship Through a Colorful Journey, Sally Collins

At Home with Patrick Lose: Colorful Quilted Projects, Patrick Lose

Beautifully Quilted with Alex Anderson: • How to Choose or Create the Best Designs for Your Quilt • 6 Timeless Projects • Full-Size Patterns, Ready to Use, Alex Anderson

Best of Baltimore Beauties, The: 95 Patterns for Album Blocks and Borders, Elly Sienkiewicz

Best of Baltimore Beauties Part II, The: More Patterns for Album Blocks, Elly Sienkiewicz

Block Magic, Too!: Over 50 NEW Blocks from Squares and Rectangles, Nancy Johnson-Srebro

Butterflies & Blooms: Designs for Appliqué & Quilting, Carol Armstrong

Cats in Quilts: 14 Purrfect Projects, Carol Armstrong

Color Play: Easy Steps to Imaginative Color in Quilts, Joen Wolfrom

Come Listen to my Quilts: •Playful Projects •Mix & Match Designs, Kristina Becker

Contemporary Classics in Plaids & Stripes: 9 Projects from Piece O' Cake Designs, Linda Jenkins & Becky Goldsmith

Crazy Quilt Handbook, The: Revised, 2nd Edition, Judith Baker Montano

Curves in Motion: Quilt Designs & Techniques, Judy Dales

Cut-Loose Quilts: Stack, Slice, Switch, and Sew, Jan Mullen

Do-It-Yourself Framed Quilts: Fast, Fun & Easy Projects, Gai Perry

Dresden Flower Garden: A New Twist on Two Quilt Classics, Blanche Young

Easy Pieces: Creative Color Play with Two Simple Quilt Blocks, Margaret Miller

Elm Creek Quilts: Quilt Projects Inspired by the Elm Creek Quilts Novels, Jennifer Chiaverini & Nancy Odom

Fancy Appliqué: 12 Lessons to Enhance Your Skills, Elly Sienkiewicz

Fantastic Fabric Folding: Innovative Quilting Projects, Rebecca Wat

Felt Wee Folk: Enchanting Projects, Salley Mavor

Four Seasons in Flannel: 23 Projects—Quilts & More, Jean Wells & Lawry Thorn

Floral Stitches: An Illustrated Guide to Floral Stitchery, Judith Baker Montano

Flower Pounding: Quilt Projects for All Ages, Ann Frischkorn & Amy Sandrin

Freddy's House: Brilliant Color in Quilts, Freddy Moran

Free Stuff for Quilters on the Internet, 3rd Edition, Judy Heim & Gloria Hansen

Free Stuff for Stitchers on the Internet, Judy Heim & Gloria Hansen

Ghost Layers and Color Washes: Three Steps to Spectacular Quilts, Katie Pasquini Masopust

Great Lakes, Great Quilts: 12 Projects Celebrating Quilting Traditions, Marsha MacDowell

Hand Appliqué with Alex Anderson: Seven Projects for Hand Appliqué, Alex Anderson

Impressionist Palette: Quilt Color & Design, Gai Perry

In the Nursery: Creative Quilts and Designer Touches, Jennifer Sampou & Carolyn Schmitz

Jacobean Rhapsodies: Composing with 28 Appliqué Designs, Pat Campbell & Mimi Ayers

Kaleidoscope Artistry, Cozy Baker

Kaleidoscopes: Wonders of Wonder, Cozy Baker

Laurel Burch Quilts: Kindred Creatures, Laurel Burch

Luscious Landscapes: Simple Techniques for Dynamic Quilts, Joyce R. Becker

Magical Four-Patch and Nine-Patch Quilts, Yvonne Porcella

Make Any Block Any Size: Easy Drawing Method, Unlimited Pattern Possibilities, Sensational Quilt Designs, Joen Wolf

Mary Mashuta's Confetti Quilts: A No-Fuss Approach to Color, Fabric & Design, Mary Mashuta

Mastering Machine Appliqué, 2nd Edition: The Complete Guide Including: • Invisible Machine Appliqué • Satin Stitch • Blanket Stitch & Much More, Harriet Hargrave

Michael James: Art & Inspirations, Michael James

New Sampler Quilt, The, Diana Leone

Paper Piecing Potpourri: Fun-Filled Projects for Every Quilter, From the Editors and Contributors of Quilter's Newsletter Magazine and Quiltmaker magazine

Paper Piecing with Alex Anderson: •Tips •Techniques •6 Projects, Alex Anderson

Patchwork Persuasion: Fascinating Quilts from Traditional Designs, Joen Wolfrom

Patchwork Quilts Made Easy—Revised, 2nd Edition: 33 Quilt Favorites, Old & New, Jean Wells

Perfect Union of Patchwork & Appliqué, A, Darlene Christopherson

Pieced Flowers, Ruth B. McDowell

Provence Quilts and Cuisine, Marie-Christine Flocard & Cosabeth Parriaud

Q is for Quilt, Diana McClun & Laura Nownes

Quick Quilts for the Holidays: 11 Projects to Stamp, Stencil, and Sew, Trice Boerens

Quilting with Carol Armstrong: •30 Quilting Patterns•Appliqué Designs•16 Projects, Carol Armstrong

Quilting with the Muppets: 15 Fun and Creative Projects, The Jim Henson Company in association with the Sesame Workshop

Quilts for Guys: 15 Fun Projects For Your Favorite Fella, edited by Cyndy Lyle Rymer

Ultimate Guide to Longarm Quilting, The: •How to Use Any Longarm Machine •Techniques, Patterns & Pantographs •Starting a Business •Hiring a Longarm Machine Quilter, Linda Taylor

Radiant New York Beauties: 14 Paper-Pieced Quilt Projects, Valori Wells

Reverse Appliqué with No Brakez, Jan Mullen

Rx for Quilters: Stitcher-Friendly Advice for Every Body, Susan Delaney-Mech

Sew Much Fun: 14 Projects to Stitch & Embroider, Oklahoma Embroidery Supply & Design

Shadow Redwork™ with Alex Anderson: 24 Designs to Mix and Match, Alex Anderson

Shoreline Quilts: 15 Glorious Get-Away Projects, compiled by Cyndy Rymer

Show Me How to Machine Quilt: A Fun, No-Mark Approach, Kathy Sandbach

Simple Fabric Folding for Christmas: 14 Festive Quilts & Projects, Liz Aneloski

Simply Stars: Quilts That Sparkle, Alex Anderson

Slice of Christmas from Piece O' Cake Designs, A, Linda Jenkins & Becky Goldsmith

Snowflakes & Quilts, Paula Nadelstern

Stripes In Quilts, Mary Mashuta

Strips 'n Curves: A New Spin on Strip Piecing, Louisa L. Smith

Thimbleberries Housewarming, A: 22 Projects for Quilters, Lynette Jensen

Visual Dance, The: Creating Spectacular Quilts, Joen Wolfrom

Wild Birds: Designs for Appliqué & Quilting, Carol Armstrong

Wildflowers: Designs for Appliqué and Quilting, Carol Armstrong

Wine Country Quilts: A Bounty of Flavorful Projects for Any Palette, Cyndy Lyle Rymer & Jennifer Rounds

For more information, write for a free catalog:
C&T Publishing, Inc.
P.O. Box 1456
Lafayette, CA 94549
(800) 284-1114
Email: ctinfo@ctpub.com
Website: www.ctpub.com

For quilting supplies:
Cotton Patch Mail Order
3405 Hall Lane, Dept.CTB
Lafayette, CA 94549
(800) 835-4418
(925) 283-7883
Email:quiltusa@yahoo.com
Website: www.quiltusa.com

NOTE: Fabrics used in the quilts shown may not be currently available since fabric manufacturers keep most fabrics in print for only a short time.